Kaiser Wilhelm II: The Life  Emperor during World War I

By Charles River Editors

About Charles River Editors

Charles River Editors was founded by Harvard and MIT alumni to provide superior editing and original writing services, with the expertise to create digital content for publishers across a vast range of subject matter. In addition to providing original digital content for third party publishers, Charles River Editors republishes civilization's greatest literary works, bringing them to a new generation via ebooks.

Introduction

Kaiser Wilhelm II in 1902

Kaiser Wilhelm II (1859-1941)

"You will be home before the leaves fall from the trees." – Kaiser Wilhelm II to German troops leaving for the front at the start of World War I.

Kaiser Friedrich Wilhelm II, who occupied the throne of the German Empire for more than 30 years from June 1888-November 1918, remains as much an enigma in death as he was in life. Over 70 years after his death in 1941, the mention of his name still sparks unsettled debates among historians. Was he the duty-bound, hands-on leader and passionate pro-British reformer who ruled in challenging times, seemingly mild by comparison with Hitler? Or was he an inept, mentally imbalanced and reckless seeker of attention? Was he even possibly a tragic hero that could only fail at his task given the complexities of his age? At the core of such diverse opinions are the contradictory assumptions found within the vast amount of scholarship that exists on the emperor and his era. On one point, however, there is agreement: his influence on imperial Germany was enormous.

The earliest writings on Wilhelm II tended to treat him either bitterly as the most hated man in Europe and an out-of-touch autocrat who mismanaged his government and left the world embroiled in the greatest war it had ever seen, or as a respectful and loyal servant of the state and faithful husband. But in the past 50 years, historiography has favored a dispassionate approach that has transcended the earlier writings' depiction of the Kaiser either slavishly or as the cause of the age's tribulations. This dispassionate trend in scholarship originated with a seminar on "Kaiser Wilhelm II as a Cultural Phenomenon", given in 1977 at the University of Freiburg by Professor John Röhl and based on his discovery of new archival materials. Two years later, Röhl and others met in Corfu and presented a series of pioneering studies about the influence of the Kaiser on German politics. Röhl believed he found in Wilhelm II the key to understanding the recklessness and downfall of Imperial Germany. The Kaiser, according to Röhl's theory, promoted the policies of naval and colonial expansion so extensively that they inevitably caused a sharp deterioration in British relations before 1914.

Given that he was a longstanding emperor of one of World War I's major combatants, it seems odd that it would take 50 years of research to come to the conclusion that the Kaiser played a major role in the march to war. But the early exculpatory research also had its arguments. In 1919, German diplomat Bernhard von Bülow removed from German archives any documents that might support the view that Germany was responsible for the war, so only documents which lessened Germany's role in bringing about World War I could be seen by researchers. From 1923-1927, the German Foreign Ministry published dozens of volumes from the archives and carefully edited them to make it appear that the war was the result of a breakdown of international relations. Holger Herwig has concluded that most if not all research on Germany's role in the First World War prior to Fritz Fischer's book *Griff nach der Weltmacht* is little more than an ideologically-driven "sham".

Kaiser Wilhelm II: The Life and Legacy of Germany's Emperor during World War I examines the life of one of the 20th century's most important rulers, and the debates over his legacy. Along with pictures of important people, places, and events, you will learn about Germany's most famous Kaiser like you never have before.

Chapter 1: Early Years

Wilhelm II and his father in 1862

Wilhelm II appeared in the world the hard way: by a painful breech birth that nearly killed him and his mother. Just before midnight on January 26, 1858, his mother went into labor and was given a sedative. The baby began to arrive the following afternoon by appearing buttocks first and had to be surgically removed. Despite the festivities and public reports of health and vigor, the doctor's report written two weeks later called the baby "seemingly dead to a high degree." To those around him, the future Kaiser appeared dead at first until he was slapped and doused with cold water.[1] Soon after the birth, nurses also noticed that the baby's left arm was nearly completely paralyzed. Believing that the ailment was temporary, Wilhelm's parents were not alarmed. Many have speculated about the effect of the child's physical limitations on his subsequent character formation; as an adult, Wilhelm's left arm remained about six inches shorter than the right and was unable to lift anything heavier than a few ounces. Throughout his life Wilhelm kept his hand hidden from photographers and perhaps as compensation developed a vice-like handshake in his right arm.

In this picture, Wilhelm is clasping his left hand with his right arm to hide the affliction.

Wilhelm II was born into the Hohenzollern family, descended from the impoverished line of the Coburgs who had ruled the duchy of Saxe-Coburg for centuries. The family had long demonstrated a great talent for marrying higher than their station, and they consistently had their eyes on British marriage partners. The first major coup occurred when Leopold of Coburg married an heiress to the British throne in 1816. That marriage, however, remained childless, with Leopold becoming a widower a year later. By 1850, however, the Coburg's strategy had resulted in marriages with the most important families of continental Europe. The greatest marital victory came in 1840 when King Leopold of the Belgians arranged a marriage between the Coburg Prince Albert and Queen Victoria of England. The Queen's mother, who happened to be King Leopold's sister, was also a Coburg, meaning Victoria and Albert were first cousins.

---

[1] Von der Kiste 6

Queen Victoria and Albert

While European marriages had traditionally been arranged ones where love was unnecessary, Wilhelm II's father, known as Fritz, did not require political machinations to marry his wife. During Fritz's second trip to England in 1855, he fell in love with Queen Victoria's oldest daughter: Victoria, Princess Royal. Victoria reciprocated his feelings immediately, and the two became engaged in September 1855, just shy of Victoria's 15th birthday. After an engagement lasting two and a half years, Fritz and Victoria married in January 1858, and moved to a new home in Germany. In January 1859, the future Wilhelm II was born.

Victoria, Wilhelm II's mother

Frederick III, Wilhelm II's father

Not long after the arrival of the child bride Victoria, the young woman became distrusted as a dangerous outsider. From the moment the nuptials were announced, the engagement was attacked as "unfortunate" in an editorial of a British newspaper, and on the Prussian side, the sentiment was not much better. The dominant viewpoint was articulated by the conservative young politician Otto von Bismarck, who in a letter stated, "If the Princess can leave the Englishwoman at home and become a Prussian, then she may be a blessing to the country. If our future Queen on the Prussian throne remains the least bit English, then I see our Court surrounded by English influence…What will it be like when the first lady in the land is an Englishwoman?"[2] Victoria likewise showed limited affection for her father-in-law Wilhelm I when he assumed the Prussian throne in early 1861. He insisted on controlling her movements, and she found him paranoid and defensive. To Victoria's dismay, the Emperor also found England uninspiring.

Victoria's fall from grace as a young mother at court was swift, and it corresponded with the rise to power of Otto von Bismarck. Bismarck was called to become minister-president in 1862 during a constitutional crisis over Prussian army reforms, and he was prepared to rule by decree.

---

[2] Van der Kiste, 3.

Bismarck threatened to overrule the legislature until it followed the Emperor Wilhelm I's lead, and when Bismarck did in fact dissolve parliament, the liberal Princess Victoria viewed him as falsely influencing the Emperor toward a more reactionary position. Long before her husband would take the throne and engage Bismarck head on, documents from the royal archives show that Victoria viewed Bismarck as a dangerous Anglophobic "troublemaker."[3] The young Wilhelm was undoubtedly aware of his mother's conflict with Bismarck and would later continue the confrontation as an adult.

Bismarck

The future Kaiser's early education was entrusted to Georg Ernst Hinzpeter, whose links to the crown, specifically Wilhelm I, guaranteed him the post. He was granted exclusive authority over the prince's education and remained in that capacity until the prince's 18th birthday. Hinzpeter set a demanding curriculum in Latin, history, religion, mathematics, and modern languages that

---

[3] Cecil, 7

lasted 12 hours a day, yet Victoria repeatedly complained about interference in educational matters from the crown. In an attempt to limit the crown's influence, she suggested sending the future Kaiser to a Gymnasium in Kassel, where he would be educated with the middle class children of his own age. No Hohenzollern prince had ever been educated in this manner, and Victoria had some success against the crown powers when she succeeded in having her son taught away from Berlin, where she viewed the Gymnasia as too reactionary.

In September 1874, young Wilhelm was confirmed in the Protestant church in Potsdam, with numerous luminaries present, including his parents and the Prince and Princess of Wales. According to his mother, the ceremony "moved him very deeply." Shortly after his confirmation, he packed for Kassel, but by all accounts, the Kaiser was not happy with the deviation from the typical traditional military training of Prussian princes. Nevertheless, he ultimately yielded to Hinzpeter, who believed that the limitations caused by Wilhelm's physical deformity would lead him to compensate via an overbearing sense of superiority.[4] There is evidence too that Wilhelm was not too happy with his middle class educational experiment; he thought the school overlooked character development and skills needed for a practical life.

Furthermore, Wilhelm resented being exposed to academic competition with members of the middle classes, at least initially. The headmaster of the school, Gideon Vogt, insisted that Wilhelm be treated like all other students, and on this point, Kaiser Wilhelm I conceded with one exception: there could be no more than 21 students in a classroom. Other students said that Wilhelm acted conceited and arrogant at first but quickly adapted and made many friends.[5] On top of that, Hinzpeter followed Wilhelm to Kassel and set up a regimen that was no less strict than his years in Berlin. Wilhelm was up before sunrise, spent the morning in studies, and quickly ate lunch so he could partake in 90 minutes of physical training. The classes continued at 2:00 p.m., and after the school day ended, Wilhelm was required to report to Hinzpeter and report all that he had learned. After dinner, the school boys worked until 8:00 p.m. which was followed by an hour or 90 minutes of tutoring.

Despite his reservations, the curriculum at Kassel focused on classical languages and Wilhelm excelled at Greek and Latin, reading the classics and identifying with the deeds of bravery in the Iliad. His favorite subject was medieval German history, and he also excelled in French, English and horsemanship.[6] Wilhelm stayed three years in Kassel, and in January 1877 he passed his university examinations with a mark of *gut* (good). Shortly thereafter, Hinzpeter resigned his position, his work complete, but looking back on his 12 years of service as tutor, Hinzpeter later told people the Kassel experiment had been a failure because the prince had not achieved all that Hinzpeter had hoped he would. This judgment may have been due at least in part to the fact Hinzpeter had developed a dislike for the prince's personality, which he saw as cold and steely.[7]

---

[4] Van der Kisten, 18
[5] Cecil, 31
[6] Cecil, 32
[7] Cecil, 35

For his part, Wilhelm II said of Hinzpeter, "Hinzpeter was really a good fellow. Whether he was the right tutor for me, I dare not decide. The torments inflicted on me, in this pony riding, must be attributed to my mother."

A mere week after Wilhelm's graduation, the Kaiser sent him off to a military career, so in February 1877 Wilhelm joined the First Foot Guards at Potsdam. Wilhelm seemed to thrive in the military atmosphere, but as his mother complained, he seemed to best enjoy his time doing nothing. Eventually, Wilhelm's parents decided to move their son out of Potsdam and send him to the university at Bonn, which would keep his mind more active.

Wilhelm's stay in Bonn lasted two years, during which he visited numerous lectures and called on professors at home. The professor who had the greatest effect on Wilhelm was Reinhard Kekule, an authority on Greek art, and Wilhelm appreciated Kekule so much that he later granted Kekule a title of nobility. Wilhelm was also regarded at Bonn as a likeable young man, albeit one with an average intellect. His teachers believed he would have done much better had he worked harder, to the extent that Wilhelm's uncle, whose son also studied at Bonn, feared that Wilhelm would be a bad influence on his son. One professor noted that what Wilhelm enjoyed the most in Bonn was the fraternity life. During his second year in Bonn, Wilhelm joined the Borussen society, the most socially exclusive of all fraternities, consisting entirely of nobility who eventually ended up as military officers. Wilhelm would later send a number of his sons to Bonn for study, where they too joined the Borussen Society.

When Wilhelm was 19, he fell in love with Princess Augusta Victoria, the daughter of Duke Friedrich of Schleswig-Holstein-Sonderburg-Augustenburg, a member of the Danish royal family. Princess Augusta Victoria's mother was a first cousin once removed from Wilhelm's grandfather, Prince Albert. There were many objections to be overcome before "Dona", as Princess Augusta Victoria was known, could be accepted at court. Although she was a noble, her father's declining fortunes and marginal royal status raised questions of suitability, and Dona was also a few months older than Wilhelm. However, this also offered some advantages, because the family's weaknesses would lead the Queen to complement her husband rather than compete with him. The family also had widespread connections and was staunchly Protestant.

Princess Augusta Victoria

Eventually, Dona won the praise of the Crown Prince Fritz, Wilhelm's father, who was delighted that the relationship was based on love rather than politics. Conversely, Wilhelm's mother had a more muted opinion, fearing that her son was too immature for marriage and preferring that he travel some more before getting married. In the end, the Crown Princess was convinced that marriage would keep Wilhelm moral, and a year after the couple was engaged, the Crown Princess reported to Queen Victoria that all objections had been overcome.[8] Dona arrived in Berlin on February 26, 1881, and became the centerpiece of a large parade. The wedding took place the next day, and for two days both bride and groom took part in ceremonies. She would remain his wife until her death four decades later in 1921, and between 1882 and

---

[8] Cecil, 50

1892, she bore Wilhelm six sons and a daughter.

During their first years of marriage, Wilhelm and Dona rarely left Potsdam. Wilhelm returned to the Foot Guards Regiment as a lieutenant and began to devote more and more time with his official duties, participating in regimental exercises and maneuvers and studying great battles of antiquity. Dona found out that she was pregnant in the late summer of 1881, and a boy named Wilhelm was born the following year. Five brothers followed: Eitel Friedrich (1883), Adalbert (1884), August Wilhelm, known as Auwi, (1887), Oskar (1888) and Joachim (1890). One daughter, Victoria Louise, was born in 1892.

Augusta Victoria and Victoria Louise

From the outside the marriage appeared to be happy, but neither Wilhelm nor Dona were without complaints. Dona admired her husband and wished never to be separated from him, but she realized that his military companions and political comrades had ultimate control over him. Wilhelm spent the early years of his marriage hunting with friends in Brandenburg and Silesia, and historian Lamar Cecil has asserted that Wilhelm maintained a series of secret affairs between the year after his marriage and shortly after he became Emperor in 1888.

Ultimately, Wilhelm sought and found the type of sanctuary in the military that counteracted what he perceived to be an overbearing mother and acquiescent father, but in doing so, he limited his social circle to his fellow officers in Potsdam. Wilhelm was swallowed up socially by a group of younger officers such as Adjutant Bernhard von Bülow, who would later become chancellor, and Wilhelm von Liebenau, who was later to become his Court Marshal. They were politically ultra conservative and believed in the Prussian military tradition, yet they secretly questioned the future Kaiser's abilities.[9] Wilhelm was accused of narrow-mindedness and was urged even by Chancellor Bismarck to relocate to Berlin, where he would have more worldly experiences.

Chapter 2: The Road to the Throne

When the future Kaiser Wilhelm II was born on January 27, 1859, his grandfather, Wilhelm I, still occupied the throne. It would be nearly 30 years before his grandfather died, passing power briefly to his son before it was transferred to Wilhelm II. Thus, for nearly three decades, Wilhelm II was prepared by various influences that would determine his ruling style. During these decades Wilhelm watched the relationship between his father and grandfather, and the influence of his grandfather cannot be overstated. Since his grandfather was Kaiser, Wilhelm's parents were always subordinated to a higher authority, and all members of the Hohenzollern family were subject to the final authority of the Kaiser Wilhelm I. The young prince's mother often complained that the children were treated like public property.[10]

---

[9] Cecil, 60
[10] Clark, 2

Kaiser Wilhelm I

When Wilhelm returned to Potsdam from his studies in Bonn, associates began to notice a close relationship forming between him and the Kaiser. Although Wilhelm rarely visited Berlin, when he did it was to visit his grandfather, and the Kaiser seemed to be satisfied that Wilhelm had shed the English influence of his mother. Even as others surrounding the Kaiser complained of a stubbornness and conceit that would demonstrate itself more forcefully when Wilhelm II became Kaiser, the Kaiser favored Wilhelm II personally. The Kaiser promoted Wilhelm to Major and sent him from the foot guards to the Guard Hussars, an elite aristocratic corps with many members from the best houses.

Despite that favorable assignment Wilhelm was known during this time for his battle against vice. Insisting that others observe his strict moral code against drinking and gambling, Wilhelm had one of the favored establishments of the Hussars placed on a list of forbidden establishments. During this time, Wilhelm also became close friends with Herbert von Bismarck, the chancellor's eldest son (though the friendship did not prevent the rupture between Wilhelm II and the elder Bismarck after Wilhelm became Kaiser). The military officers Wilhelm met and got to know during this period would play roles of great prominence after he acquired the throne.

Beginning in the fall of 1886, with Wilhelm I ailing, the Crown Prince suffered from chronic hoarseness, which often robbed him of his voice. The following March, a growth was discovered on his left vocal cord. Experts wavered on whether to operate, and ultimately the Crown Prince decided that the surgery was too risky. He preferred to live a short life on the throne than to make himself a mute, and thus uncrownable. By the middle of 1887, the Crown Prince was mortally ill with cancer, and he wailed, "To think I should have such a horrid disgusting illness ... I had so hoped to have been of use to my country." It suddenly seemed that Wilhelm II would soon ascend to the throne.

The Crown Princess was sent to San Remo in hopes the warm air would provide a curing effect, but the prospect of young Wilhelm II soon becoming Kaiser worried Chancellor Bismarck. Bismarck believed that if Wilhelm came to the throne with his current lack of experience, it was bound to be disastrous to the national interests. Until the onset of Wilhelm I's illness, Bismarck had kept his distance from the young prince. Bismarck's son Herbert served as a connection, Bismarck observed that the younger Wilhelm always treated him with respect and deference, and Wilhelm always hung on every word of the elder Bismarck. Still, even though the Bismarcks turned their attention to courting Wilhelm, Chancellor Bismarck felt Wilhelm was not ready for the throne, even if he possessed the elements capable of being molded into a sovereign, and this seemed to be an opinion shared by Wilhelm's father, who moaned just a month before his death, "I cannot die ... What would happen to Germany?"

Sure enough, the seriousness of the Crown Prince's illness suddenly thrust Wilhelm II into a new light. The Kaiser serenely took the news of his son's condition and began to make preparations for Wilhelm II's succession; as upsetting as it was to the Crown Prince and Crown Princess, he decided Wilhelm II should accept some of the burden of rule. In order to assure a smooth transition of power, on November 17, the Kaiser issued an order allowing Wilhelm general authority to serve as the representative of the Kaiser in mostly ceremonial duties. The Kaiser's also instructed Chancellor Bismarck to instruct Wilhelm II in the affairs of state. Until this point, Bismarck had not expressed much interest in Wilhelm II, and he was now faced with the unhappy prospect that the Prince would soon be his boss. Thus began a relationship between two men that would be strained at times and which would have dire consequences for the whole of Europe.

When the Kaiser passed away on March 9, 1888, the Crown Prince's ailing health prevented him from greeting the dignitaries that descended on Berlin for the Kaiser's funeral. By appearing from a window in the Charlottenburg Palace, he relieved some of his followers, but the ailing new Kaiser left all state business in the hands of Bismarck, which gave Bismarck more authority than he had ever had.

During the 99 days of Frederick III's reign, his wife lived in a near state of denial. Knowing full well the prognosis made by her husband's doctors, she hired a team of interior decorators from London to refurbish Charlottenburg Palace. In public, she remained cheerful, leading her enemies in Berlin to claim that she was on the threshold of madness.[11] Meanwhile, Victoria suspected many courtiers, especially Bismarck, of conspiring against the couple and depriving them of power by treating Wilhelm II as the true Kaiser. In turn, the dislike Wilhelm II had for his mother was only intensified by his father's short reign, and by the time Frederick III passed away, the rift between mother and son was so deep that it could hardly be mended.

Bismarck watched with delight as the relationship between mother and son deteriorated, for he knew that he needed to begin to influence the future ruler long before the young Wilhelm took over the throne. Bismarck and his son, however, would learn that the Prince had an independent streak. The first great break with Bismarck came after Wilhelm expressed a desire for a war against Russia; Wilhelm held increasingly hostile views toward Russia ever since his second visit there in 1886, and anti-German feeling was prevalent in Russia because of Bismarck's support of Austria to the Russians' disadvantage in the Balkans. However, Bismarck was not willing to share Wilhelm's lust for war, because he was familiar with the complexities of internal Russian politics and did not see war as an inevitable result. Wilhelm shot back by publicly repudiating Bismarck's policy toward Russia and Austria, and though Bismarck retorted privately to a friend that he had no intention of going to war with Russia, in public he claimed that a war with Russia was a possibility. All the while, the Chancellor and the Crown Prince began drifting apart.

Frederick III began his agonizing death on June 14, 1888. By that point, the cancerous growth on his throat broke through the skin and he could no longer eat. He refused artificial nourishment and died around noon the following day.

Chapter 3: The New Emperor

Wilhelm's first act as the new Kaiser was to address the Prussian army, a fittingly symbolic choice since it set the tone of his whole reign and made clear military affairs would be the supreme expression of his interests. And as he had demonstrated earlier, he continued to battle vice. One of the first acts of the new sovereign was to wage a campaign against the drinking clubs popular among the officer corps; only a few weeks after assuming the throne, Wilhelm II ordered army commanders to prevent all army officers from frequenting such clubs.

The Kaiser then proceeded to tackle more serious matters. In the summer of 1888, acting on his

---

[11] Cecil, 113

belief that the officers' ranks were getting on in years, Wilhelm began to cull the ranks of the more elderly and feeble officers, leading to accusations that he was micromanaging who received key posts.[12] For example, Wilhelm appointed his long-time friend, General Count von Waldersee, as Chief of the General Staff, and the two began to make changes to numerous military positions. Part of what made General Count von Waldersee attractive to Wilhelm was his staunch anti-Russian attitude. In the same vein, Wilhelm insulated himself by his tendency to appoint likable officers as his adjutants, and in reference to these elegant soldiers who were chosen for their appearance and social standing, later chancellor Prince Hohenlohe would call them the "Chinese wall." Wilhelm was also accused of taking revenge on officers who opposed him well before he ascended the throne.

Wilhelm listened more eagerly to fellow officers than to civilians, and in the early years of his reign, military matters almost entirely consumed him, causing Victoria to complain that her family had been destroyed.[13] The Kaiser even participated in regimental exercises two or three times a week, an enthusiasm for the army that was also problematic for Bismarck too because it gave enormous influence to Wilhelm's military cronies. Bismarck feared that this group was ignorant of anything other than military affairs, and on top of that, Count von Waldersee ordered military attaches in foreign capitals to report directly to him, thus meddling in Bismarck's diplomacy. Waldersee sought to create a military network independent of Bismarck's diplomatic channels.

Wilhelm's focus on military matters and his tendency to take advice and direction exclusively from a small coterie of military men had other effects as well. Even though he would end up ruling for 30 years, historians have pointed out that his connection with his subjects was weak and narcissistic. The sovereign was insulated from the realities of Imperial Germany by the fact that he had a very small group of close confidants, all of whom were dependent on the throne for their positions.

Nevertheless, Wilhelm sought to be the ruler of all his subjects despite that insulation, and in the early years of his reign, Wilhelm introduced reforms aimed at expanding his base of support. He made plans to open up the officer corps to the middle-classes, and he also appointed notable progressives to high profile posts in the military.[14] Through these measures, Wilhelm enjoyed considerable popularity with the working class, at least in the beginning. For a while, he was perceived as "the workers' King." It was due to the influence of Wilhelm's early tutor Hinzpeter that the young Kaiser paid such attention to the lower social classes. The Kaiser believed that government must grant concessions to the poor as an antidote to Bismarck's repressive labor policies, and Wilhelm II was only Kaiser for less than a year before his ideas were tested. Strikes began in the coal industry in the Rhineland and in Silesia in May 1889, leading Prussian troops

---

[12] Cecil I, pg 125
[13] Cecil, 128
[14] Cecil, 133

to quell the violence. Wilhelm believed the strikes were caused by Polish Catholic fanatics, whom historians now say bore only part of the responsibility. Wilhelm's opinion was that the entire Rhineland had been neglected by the industrialists as soon as they made their quick profits. The Rhineland industrialists did not, in Wilhelm's opinion, create favorable conditions like those that existed in the state factories of Silesia, and Wilhelm was determined not to begin his reign with bloodshed. Thus, he ordered his military to protect workers against employers, which he believed was the only way to decrease the incidence of labor violence.

On the same front, the Kaiser allowed the first deputation of workers to visit the palace to express their grievances and expectations for an 8 hour work day. The Kaiser urged the industrialists to negotiate with labor, which led to a settlement within two weeks, and Wilhelm took great relish in the fact that he had been the cause of the agreement.[15] On the other hand, Bismarck was horrified; in his mind, the working class could never be appeased and had to be coerced into its proper position. Bismarck rejected the Kaiser's insistence that the working classes be brought on board the planning of social programs as equal participants. Although he had created social welfare legislation that was unique for Europe at the time, Bismarck believed the state should act repressively in the wake of socialist electoral victories. Bismarck was waging what he viewed as preventative class warfare.

Chapter 4: The Rift with Bismarck and the Power Vacuum

The disagreement over how to deal with the strike in the Rhineland and Silesia was merely the first major argument between the two powerful personalities. The first conflict before an audience of public officials took place on May 12, 1889, at a meeting of ministers. Bismarck held that the situation should be allowed to worsen in order to allow a pretext for more sweeping action against the agitators, but the Kaiser expressed his viewpoint that the demands of the workers should be considered since any further worsening of the situation would weaken the Empire. As that debate made clear, it was apparent from the beginning that the chancellor would need to handle his boss carefully. The Kaiser obviously intended to be the dominant force in both domestic and foreign policy, and the chancellor quickly learned that he would have to adapt to the Kaiser's demands on every day matters.

However, after spending decades as the de facto dictator of the empire, Bismarck found it difficult to relinquish power. The year 1890 began with the two figures still arguing over policies toward workers, and the two squared off over the contents of the Kaiser's speech to open the parliament's annual meeting. The Kaiser insisted on appeasing the coalition of Social Democrats and their Catholic allies with a new round of socially progressive legislation that would protect the working class, while Bismarck's response was that he would rather resign than give in to the Social Democrats. The Kaiser opined to his confidants that the chancellor had become increasingly difficult to deal with, but the Kaiser still needed Bismarck to help assure passage of

---

[15] Cecil, 135

an increasingly large military budget later in the spring.

On January 24, the Kaiser opened the parliament with a detailed speech on the labor question; the miners' strikes of the previous year in the Rhineland had created an atmosphere that had to be dealt with. The Kaiser admitted that the explosive growth of German industry had allowed exploitative publicly traded companies to come into existence, mistreating workers and pushing them into the willing arms of agitators. The success of socialist agitators was due, said the Kaiser, to government's inability to providing reforming labor legislation. The Kaiser struck a middle line by saying that the government must pass progressive legislation on the side of the working man without tolerating exorbitant demands that would injure Germany's ability to compete on the world market. In the same speech, he rejected the demands for an 8 hour work day and a 50% increase in wages that had been demanded by miners in the Rhineland.

As expected, Bismarck's response to the speech was negative, and by the end of January 1890, the Kaiser had reached a decision on a replacement for Bismarck. He called General Leo von Caprivi, the commanding general of the Tenth Army Corps, to Berlin and told Caprivi that in the event of a final break with Bismarck, Caprivi would be his desired successor. Meanwhile, by mid-February, Bismarck was hoping for an opportunity to use the ever growing possibility of a coup d'etat as a pretext for setting aside the constitution of 1871 and disbanding parliament. Recently held elections weakened Bismarck's position and required that in the future he make amends with the Catholic Center and Social Democrats, but the fear of a coup was not enough to put Bismarck and the Kaiser back on equal footing. As historian Michael Balfour put it in *The Kaiser and his Times*, when Bismarck was aware that time was running out on him, "All Bismarck's resources were deployed; he even asked Empress Victoria to use her influence at her son on his behalf. But the wizard had lost his magic; his spells were powerless because they were exerted on people who did not respect them, and he who had so signally disregarded Kant's command to use people as ends in themselves had too small a stock of loyalty to draw on. As Lord Salisbury told Queen Victoria: 'The very qualities which Bismarck fostered in the Emperor in order to strengthen himself when the Emperor Frederick should come to the throne have been the qualities by which he has been overthrown.' The Empress, with what must have been a mixture of pity and triumph, told him that her influence with her son could not save him for he himself had destroyed it."

Despite the advice of advisers that he should sack the chancellor, the Kaiser was hesitant to do so. Wilhelm was concerned about public opinion and the passage of the military budget, but due to an ongoing dispute over a document that the Kaiser requested from Bismarck, Bismarck submitted his resignation on March 19. Wilhelm was finally finished with the chancellor.

A famous political cartoon, titled "Dropping the Pilot", depicts Bismarck leaving the ship (of state) while Wilhelm II looks on from the deck.

The incoming Chancellor Caprivi was well aware of the difficulties he would face as chancellor, and the greatest of his concerns was the temperament of the Kaiser.[16] Not long after assuming office, Caprivi found that the Kaiser often charted his own course without consulting others, and after he left the office four years later, Caprivi noted that the personality of the Kaiser had been the greatest source of difficulty in the post. That said, for all Caprivi's difficulties, he and the Kaiser were largely of one mind on policy matters. Given Caprivi's lack of experience in diplomacy, he rarely challenged the Kaiser's personalized style of international politics, and

---

[16] Cecil, 173

when the two did clash it was largely over internal matters. Known as "the New Course," Caprivi's policies sought to retract imperial claims abroad in order to focus on social peace at home.

Caprivi

One of the greatest policy reversals to come after Bismarck's downfall concerned Russia. When Wilhelm became Kaiser, Germany and Russia were engaged in the "Reinsurance Treaty," a product of the Bismarck's diplomacy that required each partner to come to the assistance of the other in the event of an attack by Austria-Hungary or France. Caprivi came out against the treaty, but Wilhelm initially supported continuing it beyond the date at which it would lapse in June 1890. Many of the Kaiser's supporters urged him not to renew the treaty, and the Kaiser, believing in the power of his personal diplomacy with Russia's Tsar Alexander III, allowed the treaty to lapse.

In the area of domestic policy, the Kaiser and Caprivi agreed on the strategy of placating the working class through reform, but there were minor differences between the two. While both sought to weaken socialism by reform, the Kaiser thought the reforms should be seen as the gift of the crown, while Caprivi believed in building institutions that would design policies independent of any one person.[17] Not surprisingly, Caprivi's intention of putting the reforms in the hands of ministers and state secretaries did not appeal to Wilhelm, who sought control over all bureaucrats.

One of the key areas in which the Kaiser sought to preempt socialism was reform of the education system. The schools were to teach that socialism was an impractical social organization that contradicted Christianity, and schools were to teach that socialist governments were harmful both to the individual and to the social fabric of society. The Kaiser believed that religious instruction provided the key to weakening socialism, and teachers were to be placed under particular scrutiny. Though he was less inclined to seek changes in the education system, Caprivi acquiesced in the Kaiser's plans in order to appease the Catholic Center, so he drafted a bill that would establish separate elementary schools for Protestants and Catholics. The Kaiser, feeling that he had not been adequately consulted in the writing of the new bill, sought to have it withdrawn from consideration by the lower house of the Prussian legislature, which incensed Caprivi and spurred him to offer his resignation. That offer threw Wilhelm into such a fit of excitement that he required the intervention of the royal physician. The Kaiser eventually persuaded Caprivi to reconsider his resignation, and the education reform bill was permanently tabled in a committee of the legislature.

Although it eventually came to naught, reform of the school system was just one of the Kaiser's attempted areas of change upon coming to power in 1888. Another area in which he sought change was in the education of military cadets. Wilhelm II believed that the education of cadets should be made more practical, with less emphasis on ancient history and dead languages, and in 1890 he ordered that cadets should be drawn from the middle classes as well as the nobility. He believed that increasing the number of cadets drawn from the middle classes would insure their support against his anti-socialist measures. Furthermore, both Wilhelm and Caprivi believed in incrementally increasing the size of the army, out of fear of a backlash in the legislature should the army's size be increased too rapidly. However, the Kaiser and Caprivi came to loggerheads once again over the length of military service; the Kaiser objected to Caprivi's plan to reduce the term of service from three to two years in exchange for an increase in the number of troops, and once again the chancellor threatened to resign. The Kaiser insisted on both increases in troop levels and the continuation of a three-year term of service.

Eventually the numerous differences which divided the Kaiser and Caprivi came to a head, because the chancellor's repetitive threats of resignation were vexing to the Kaiser. In 1894, the two came to a stalemate when the president of the French republic was assassinated at the hands of an anarchist and Wilhelm gave an incendiary speech denouncing Social Democrats which was counterproductive in Caprivi's view. Wilhelm lamented the growing power of Social Democrats and their continued victories in electoral politics, and he increasingly began to view his

---

[17] Cecil, 194

attempted appeasement of the working class and his education reforms as a failure.

Throughout 1892 and 1893, worker unrest increased with strikes in the coal mining regions of the Saar, a development that the Kaiser took personally as an affront to his authority. The Kaiser backed away from his conciliatory approach to labor and sought tougher laws against the socialists, even though those laws were unlikely to pass a parliamentary vote. At this point, the Kaiser even considered dissolving parliament and calling for new elections, but when Caprivi refused to do so, the Kaiser backed down and instructed Caprivi to draft a more moderate anti-socialist law that would be acceptable to parliament. Nevertheless, Caprivi's lack of support among his ministers and the Kaiser's support of one of his rivals led the chancellor to the conclusion that he must resign, and this time the Kaiser accepted the resignation and began looking for a replacement. He found one in the person of Prince Chlodwig zu Hohenlohe-Schillingsfürst, a 75 year old Bavarian Catholic whose brother was a Cardinal.

Prince Chlodwig zu Hohenlohe-Schillingsfürst

The Kaiser believed he had found a pliant servant in the person of Hohenlohe, who shared the Kaiser's mistrust of parliament and sought tactical victories with the Kaiser and parliament rather than victories based on principle.[18] But as with Bismarck and Caprivi, the period of enchantment was brief; Hohenlohe was soon to experience the unpredictable nature of the Kaiser, especially in the area of diplomacy and in the treatment of parliament. Wilhelm repeatedly used the press to express his distaste at the Reichstag and proposed to Hohenlohe that it be dissolved.[19]

Five years into his rule, it became apparent to observers that the Kaiser was easily bored with

---

[18] Cecil, 213
[19] Cecil, 224

the details of rule, and that he preferred pageantry and the superficial benefits of authority to long hours of work at his desk before documents. The Kaiser based most of his decisions on emotions, and historian Lamar Cecil has argued that many of his projects can be traced to vanity or ego. These include the renunciation of his British mother, the implementation in the 1890s of a reactionary program, and the ambitious construction of an enormous Navy

Chapter 5: Navy and Diplomacy

The most serious political crisis of the 1890s occurred in 1895 when the Kaiser and his ministers argued over a proposed reform of the military that would allow courts martial to be held in public. Known as the Köller Affair, after the arch-conservative Interior Minister Ernst von Köller, who was accused of leaking details of confidential deliberations on the courts martial question, it is seen as a turning point in the Kaiser's reign. Ever since his appointment, Köller saw himself as a staunch supporter of the Kaiser, and his leaking of information was meant to defend the power of the crown against the proposed reform, but Köller's enemies and other ministers prevailed upon him to resign and then pressured the Kaiser to accept the resignation. In the short term, the outcome of the Köller affair seemed to be a victory for the faction which sought to check the Kaiser's control, but the victory was brief. Over time, it was clear the ministers were much too dependent on the good will of the Kaiser to mount a prolonged challenge.

Throughout the 1890s, Wilhelm's attention increasingly turned toward the Navy, which is no surprise because he had always shown an interest in ships and the sea even from an early age. Some of his first toys were miniature ships that his parents allowed him to set sail in the many parks in Berlin, and even before assuming the throne, Wilhelm oversaw the construction of a royal yacht, the expense of which became a thorny issue between him and Bismarck. As Kaiser, Wilhelm II sought changes in the Navy that were no less all-encompassing than that which he envisioned for the Army.

While Wilhelm's enthusiasm for the Navy can be seen from the beginning of his reign, it was only in the 1890s that his desire for an immense fleet became apparent. Early in his reign, he expressed his desire that England continue to rule the waves, if only to check the power of Russia and France, but the constant rebuffs at the hands of England led him to conclude that he had no other choice but to expand his own Navy. Recognizing that an Imperial Navy was essential to Bismarck's foreign policy success, two important naval advisors came on board. The first was Admiral Friedrich Hollmann, the state secretary of the imperial Naval Office, and the second was Hollmann's adjutant Admiral Gustav von Senden-Bibran, Chief of the Naval Cabinet. Both were accused of being too subservient to their masters.

The Kaiser's desire for an immense fleet came about gradually throughout the 1890s and was mirrored by the gradual acceptance of the idea of Germany as a naval power among his subjects. A number of international incidents during the first five years of Wilhelm II's rule led the Kaiser to believe that he could not rely on England to come to Germany's defense, but the Kaiser's opinion shifted radically after the Transvaal crisis in late 1895. In the Transvaal crisis, tensions brewed between the British-controlled Cape Colony and the nearby Boer South African Republic known as Transvaal; while the British had always recognized Transvaal as an independent state, Cecil Rhodes, the leading figure in the Boer Republic, called for annexation in order to take advantage of the vast gold deposits believed to be located there. Germany, however, owned one-fifth of the foreign capital invested in Transvaal, and the government in Berlin took a firm stance against annexation. Wilhelm briefly considered a war with England in Africa but was called off by his ministers and was instead convinced to send a telegram to Paul Kruger, the president of the Transvaal Republic, congratulating him on his victory in fending off the attackers. The telegram only exacerbated tensions between Berlin and London, exposing what Wilhelm believed was Britain's arrogant and dismissive treatment of Berlin. Wilhelm ultimately withdrew from the confrontation with Great Britain over the states of southern Africa, but the conflict left the Kaiser resolved to provide for Germany's defense on the seas. Since it was ultimately a lack of naval power that made it impossible to challenge British plans in South Africa, Wilhelm turned to the seas as an area to be controlled.

It wasn't only concerns about British aspirations that ignited the Kaiser's dormant interest in naval power. Wilhelm was just as concerned about the rising power of the Americans, whose naval aspirations, he believed, were being driven by British motives. The Kaiser's naval aspirations should also be viewed in light of his ongoing worry about a two front war with France and Russia, since a war on two fronts would undoubtedly have a maritime dimension. Even when Germany conquered France in 1870-71, the French navy had succeeded in blockading the coast, and in that conflict, Russia supplied grain to Germany. In the case of a true two front war, however, Germany would need to be able to sustain itself with imports and foods without relying on Russia. While America might be persuaded to be the source of imports, they would need to be transported past blockades, and this would require a powerful navy.

The implementation of the Kaiser's plans for a larger navy fell to Chancellor Hohenlohe, who agreed with the Kaiser that the protection of commerce required a larger navy, made no less necessary because Germany's recent receiving of colonies that could only be administered with a naval presence. The question was how best to obtain a large navy from a parliament historically hostile to the idea. Hohenlohe urged gradual increases in appropriations year over year rather than more drastic measures proposed by some naval officers. Members of the Reichstag had a variety of reasons to urge restraint; they did not wish to alarm Britain with drastic increases in the naval budget and they were concerned about the costs, which would be financed by taxes and thus be unpopular.

Until the mid 1890s, all factions of the parliament were hostile to the idea of a substantially larger navy. Each faction had its own reason, and the combined effect was to convince all parties involved in the naval expansion project to take a cautious approach. Two lines of thought emerged. A cruiser-based navy was proposed by some advocates within the naval establishment, while a destroyer-based navy also had some adherents. Wilhelm played both factions against one another, urging them to put forth their best plans, but in the end he supported the idea of building at least 36 new cruisers. His reasoning differed little from his overall theory of governance. Cruisers could be deployed around the world, where they would give Germany a presence, while larger battleships moored in North Sea ports to counter the influence of England offered less in the way of showmanship for the rest of the world. In the end, deputies of the parliament, eager to cut the Emperor down to size but restricted in what they could do openly by law and custom, found their method in attacking the naval plans. The budget committee rejected the requested 70 million mark budget and passed one with a total of 58 million, close to that of the preceding year.

Until the imperial fleet was inaugurated in 1898 and its eventual growth in the following decade was realized, Wilhelm would have to negotiate his way through a diplomatic minefield. The first crisis concerned China, where Russia and England held numerous interests. Germany had significant economic interests in China, and Wilhelm's squadron off the coast needed a refueling port. At risk of alienating the Russian Tsar, Wilhelm ordered the German squadron to drop anchor in an unimproved harbor and claim it for Germany. This happened completely without a negative response, and Germany ended up securing a 99 year lease for the port. However, Wilhelm's consequent undertakings, including intervening in the Turkish-Greek war, did not turn out as well as his Chinese venture, and the Kaiser continued to take diplomatic failures as a personal affront. Observers noted that the Kaiser's tirades were increasingly irrational and not based on careful analysis of any situation.[20]

By the late 1890s, rumors abounded about Wilhelm's mental health being unstable, perhaps an inheritance from his maternal and paternal lines. His reckless mind was often attributed to Hinzpeter's early education or sometimes described as a Hohenzollern attribute, but either way, everyone observed he had a difficult temper. At court, it was well known that the Kaiser's outbursts reduced numerous people to tears, including everyone from servants to military attaches, and if he lost a match of tennis, he would angrily fling his racket and go on a tirade. He would speak in such a revolting manner about other nations and their leaders that his listeners did not know what to make of it, and in public he would often make bombastic statements that had to be softened for publication. Many prominent figures, most notably Chancellor Chlodwig Hohenlohe, Admiral Alfred von Tirpitz and Ambassador Adolf Marshall von Bieberstein, were concerned about the Kaiser's mental condition.[21]

When Wilhelm appointed Bernhard von Bülow as chancellor in 1900, relations between London and Berlin were at a low point. Germany resented England's preeminence in world markets, and England was concerned about Germany's growing navy. The only thing that pulled these two powers together was their shared concerns about France and Russia. Bülow's barely concealed contempt for England matched that of his boss, and Bülow succeeded in increasing the

---

[20] Cecil, 325
[21] Cecil II, 64

Kaiser's contempt for England by convincing him that any criticism he received in the British press was a thinly veiled contempt toward his majesty. Wilhelm was also stung by the criticism emanating from his British relatives.

Bülow

Perhaps not surprisingly, Bülow would later claim after his fall from office in 1909 that the Kaiser was wholly unsuited to diplomacy. The Kaiser's vanity and indiscretions were well known, but perhaps none topped the Kaiser's relationships with England. Complaining that he had for years sought the hand of England only to be snubbed, the Kaiser took personal offense at every setback in policy. He did irreconcilable damage to international relations and his own reputation in the Daily Telegraph crisis. While traveling in England, the Kaiser granted an interview at Highcliffe Castle in November 1907, and in that interview, the Kaiser remarked that he had provided England with strategic advice during the Boer War and had prevented other continental powers from taking advantage of the Boer crisis by joining against England. He described the British as "mad, mad as march hares" for interpreting the Kaiser's desire for a larger Navy in anything other than a peaceful manner. While he admitted that the prevailing sentiment in Germany was not friendly toward Britain, he argued that he was a true friend of

England, one who always sought to strengthen relations.

When the interview was published in German, a sense of despair took hold among the German public, but especially within the Reichstag. Seething with rage and offended by a deep sense of shame, the parliament used the issue to question Wilhelm's role in politics. There was a consensus that the Kaiser had gone too far and must be reined in. The debate became evidence of a virtually complete condemnation of Wilhelm and the role of the House of Hollenzollern. The chancellor replied tepidly during questioning before the body that Wilhelm should be recognized for his long-standing attempts to foster good will between Germany and Britain, and Bülow was able to obtain from the Kaiser consent to a statement that acknowledged his obligation to behave with constitutional responsibility. The crisis was emotionally taxing on the Kaiser; for several days he was confined to bed and prescribed massages, bicarbonate of soda, and baths filled with pine needles. Wilhelm recovered and took a full month vacation from the affairs of state, only to come back and immediately sack Bülow and replace him with a little known bureaucrat named Theobald von Bethmann Hollweg.

Bethmann

Like his predecessors, Bethmann watched as his initial relationship with the Kaiser deteriorated due to the Kaiser's troublesome personality, lack of tact, and emotional volatility. Bethmann also deplored the Kaiser's tendency to close himself off with trusted courtiers who rejected the initiatives of all but the Kaiser himself. This did not make the domestic situation that the chancellor faced any easier. The first act that Bethmann undertook involved reform of the Prussian constitution to lessen the power of the landed estates by extending the franchise of voting, but the bill failed without the Kaiser's support.

Meanwhile, the growing German fleet continued to create havoc in the domestic sphere as it consumed millions of marks, and internationally the fleet was perceived as a hostile act by Great Britain. The greatest challenge for Bethmann between 1909 and 1914 involved improving relations between the two countries while at the same time growing the Navy. Bethmann understood that one of his greatest impediments to improving relations with Great Britain laws the Kaiser himself. Wilhelm II believed that a powerful German navy was a deterrent to war with Great Britain, and he believed that the two nations' economic competition would not lead to war. Wilhelm figured that as long as Germany obtained access to trade at British ports, the British could colonize the world for all he cared.

Only a month after taking office, Bethmann sought to enter into negotiations over a naval and diplomatic agreement with Britain that would put an end to the arms race. The British had raised plans in 1909 to enlarge their navy beyond the limits set in 1905 when the British government approved the plans to build Dreadnought-class battleships, and the Kaiser interpreted the British stance in negotiation as an attempt to dictate the terms of an agreement personally to the Kaiser. The British response towards Bethmann's overture was as tepid as the Kaiser's.

The original negotiations in 1909 came to naught, but the issue came up once again in 1912. This time, the Kaiser was more receptive to the idea of an agreement with Great Britain, but eventually Germany's refusal to cut back on its naval expansion plans created an insurmountable obstacle for London. The Kaiser was incensed that he was, as he put it, baited into negotiations by incompetent diplomats. His rhetoric raised the specter of war, which caused those around him once again to question his judgment; Bethmann later asserted Germany could have reached an agreement with England if not for the personal intervention of the Kaiser.

While Wilhelm was obsessed with England, especially when it came to military matters, he found protection in his alliance with the Habsburg Empire, which had been orchestrated by Bismarck in 1879. For decades, and certainly since the ascent of Wilhelm II to the throne, Austria-Hungary alone maintained unstrained relations with Germany, and unlike his reputation in other capitals, the Kaiser was highly regarded in Vienna, where his support was considered essential for shoring up the ever-weakening position of the Habsburgs. The Habsburg Empire was threatened the most by the demands of Slavic minorities on its margins, and should the

Empire dissolve, which was often rumored to be imminent, it would leave Germany with fewer allies. The Hohenzollern-Habsburg alliance was especially threatened by Russia's interests in the Balkans, where the Habsburgs occupied Bosnia and Herzegovina. Especially sensitive was the issue of Russian warships' access to the straights at Constantinople.

The Kaiser spoke openly about the need to support Austria, even to the extent of going to war if necessary against Russia. To the Kaiser, Russia's goal of claiming the Austrian Empire's Slavic subjects for Bosnia was an example of the danger which faced Europe; Wilhelm saw the Slavs as not only the cause of the potential fall of the Habsburg Empire but also as an inferior race. Serbia, in the Kaiser's eyes, was constantly stirring up trouble, and in the years leading up to war in 1914, Wilhelm assured the Habsburgs that he was ready to intervene on behalf of Austria in the case of war between Austria and the Slavic powers. The military pact between Austria and Germany was as strong as possible in the Kaiser's eyes, but his calculation of Austrian military prowess was just as overestimated as the inflated appraisal of his own abilities.

Chapter 6: World War I

While the Kaiser was full of bluster about war, he was actually convinced that war abroad was dangerous as long as the socialists presented a threat at home. In 1912, he allegedly told Bülow that war abroad was only realistic after socialists at home had been "beheaded."[22] By 1914, however, events would change that opinion.

European powers had spent much of the 19th century engaged in imperialism across the world, and their natural response was to establish alliances that would maintain at least a balance of power. When Bismarck formed an alliance with Austria-Hungary and Russia, the French subsequently signed alliances with Britain and Russia, which had left its previous alliance over tension brought about by Austria-Hungary's intervention in the Balkans. By then, Italy had joined the German alliance.

The Kaiser was aboard his yacht, the *Hohenzollern*, on the afternoon of June 28, 1914, when the telegram arrived announcing the assassination of the Archduke Franz Ferdinand and his wife in Sarajevo, the capital of Austrian Bosnia. The assassination of the heir to the Austrian throne had been carried out by Serbian nationalists, and both the Austrians and the Kaiser believed the time had come to deal decisively with Serbia. The Kaiser and chancellor von Bülow surmised that if the government in Serbia could be found responsible for the assassination, it would be a just cause for a war, and Wilhelm was actively engaged in war preparations from this time to the actual invasion of Luxembourg on August 2.

Although the assassination was a matter of local politics in the Balkans, the Kaiser took the assassination of the Archduke as a personal insult, and he felt Serbia had to be punished. The view was shared by the Austrian sovereign Franz Joseph, who urged the "elimination" of Serbia

---

[22] Cecil II, 193

in a letter to the Kaiser.[23] The Kaiser called his military staffs on July 5 to ask them if all military options remained open should Austria decide to take action, and the staff assured them that Germany could fulfill any commitments the Kaiser made to Austria. Although Wilhelm urged Austria to take strong action, it is not clear that he expected the situation to lead to a war that brought in the other European nations; Wilhelm believed that an unwillingness to fight among the French and Russians would lead to a quick resolution of hostilities as a local matter between Austria and the Serbs.

On July 19, after learning that Austria was prepared to give Serbia a forceful ultimatum, Wilhelm took great precautions to prepare Germany for war. On the 28th, Wilhelm received news that the Serbs has acquiesced to most but not all of Austria's demands, and when Vienna found the Serb reply unacceptable and declared war on Serbia later on the same day, the Kaiser cancelled his planned vacation to his castle at Wilhelmshöhe. The Austrians commenced shelling Belgrade later that day.

Despite Wilhelm's reported sense of agitation in the weeks following the assassination, and his apparent readiness for war, during the weeks following the outbreak of World War I, Wilhelm convinced himself that the situation could be resolved with diplomacy. He thought the supposed slow mobilization of forces provided time for negotiations and cooler heads to prevail, and he also looked toward the moderating influence of England, who held some sway over its French and Russian allies. However, all communications from England indicated that it held Germany responsible for the actions of Austria.[24]

As Germany descended into war with the invasion of Luxembourg on August 2, all thoughts turned to Wilhelm's role as commander in chief. Wilhelm had always said that should the fatherland go to war, he would play the decisive role as the nation's chief warlord, but after the outbreak of hostilities Wilhelm promised that he would not micromanage military operations. Courtiers noticed that the Kaiser's mood changed after the outbreak of war, so eventually he was only shown optimistic reports while the bad news was suppressed.[25] Wilhelm complained that he was kept at bay, but the Kaiser, who before 1914 saw himself as the supreme authority on peace and war, was cast aside as irresponsible and untrustworthy when the hour of need arrived.

While the Kaiser did not directly manage troop movements or question the judgment of his top generals, he frequently expressed his prediction that France would fall quickly, perhaps within two weeks. When General Erich Ludendorff swept into Belgium and captured the fortress of Liège after a difficult fight, the Kaiser claimed the war was nearly over, and that the newly acquired land would be parceled up and resettled by German soldiers and officers. Critics claimed that the Kaiser changed his war goals from day to day, never developing a clear idea of what the postwar German borders should look like, with the exception of what might transpire in

---

[23] Cecil II, 200
[24] Cecil II, 204
[25] Cecil II, 211

the east.[26] The Kaiser expressed to his son Oskar a grander scheme for German expansion in the east that would have implications for many decades to come. The Kaiser envisioned making a Polish state out of Russian territory which would be governed by a German prince, while Germany would absorb the Baltic provinces of Lithuania, Latvia, and Estonia. He had much the same visions for the Russian territories that Germany would occupy throughout the war.

Of course, the Kaiser and his leaders were surprised by the strong opposition put up by the unprepared Belgian civilian population, and that delay allowed the British and the French to begin constructing an elaborate system of trenches that would be used throughout the four-year war. The victories of August 1914 were not repeated in September, and in the middle of that month the southern flank of the German army retreated to the Marne while the northern flank continued its march toward the coast in the hopes of taking Calais. This created a disaster in the city of Ypres, where after a two-week onslaught witnessed personally by the Kaiser, the Germans were forced to retreat. The medieval city was destroyed, and 80,000 soldiers were killed.

After the Ypres fiasco, the Kaiser agreed with his advisors that resources from the eastern front should be repositioned in the west, which proved just how urgent the situation was because the Russian army at one point was within 100 miles of Berlin. When the German armies under Hindenburg and Ludendorf completed their counter attack, they achieved two of the greatest Germany victories of the war, one at Tannenberg at the end of August and later at the Masurian Lakes, where the Russian forces were nearly completely destroyed. Nevertheless, as the year 1914 drew to a close, Germany's original plan of a lightning victory in the west followed by a concentration on the eastern front was now in shambles.

As the ultimate authority in Germany, it was up to Wilhelm to resolve numerous debates, not just within the military establishment but also debates between the military and civilian powers. The diplomatic corps believed that strategic planning for war and war aims should be the work of diplomats, a role that the military was unlikely to relinquish. The role of Kaiser Wilhelm after 1914, therefore, was one of a supreme judge who was presented plans and programs which he could endorse or veto. At the same time, the Kaiser was in some ways a throwback to the past when it came to the sense of chivalry that the war would bring. When the subject of unrestrained submarine warfare came up, the Kaiser was at first clear in his position. Late in November 1914, he addressed a group of bankers and insisted that the Empire's swords must remain clean. "Always realize that our swords must be clean. We are not waging war against women and children. We wish to fight this war as gentlemen, no matter what the other side may do."[27]

Nevertheless, Wilhelm eventually agreed with his advisors that the sale of munitions to Germany's enemies by means of passenger cruise lines must stop. In February 1915, he reluctantly agreed to a policy of unrestricted naval warfare against commercial shipping. All

---

[26] Cecil II, 214
[27] Cecil II, 221

ships believed to be carrying military equipment to Germany's enemies were a fair target. This policy would have huge consequences on America's stance during World War I.

Although the U.S. was officially neutral at the beginning of the war, by winter 1914 the nation was already upset with one of the sides: the Allied Powers. Under international maritime law, navies in a state of war could only seize merchant ships not flying the enemy's flag if they had reason to believe the ships were aiding or supplying the enemy. Of course, the Allied Powers had no reason to think that of American merchant ships, but both sides were maintaining tight blockades or attempting to from the outset. Britain sought to blockade German goods, while Germany sought, less successfully, to do the same against British imports and exports. In the beginning, the Allied powers' conventional naval superiority was used to blockade the continent, while the Germans relied on their innovative U-boat submarines to harass Allied commerce. This had a material effect on the U.S., which by maintaining neutrality sought to trade with the European nations but found itself unable to because of the war. President Wilson protested that both nations stop blockading neutral countries' ships, and he even had his ambassador to Britain lodge an official protest.

His calls went unheeded, though the Germans did agree to restrict submarine warfare against American ships. But the Germans made waves in the U.S. with the 1915 sinking of the British cruise liner HMS *Lusitania*, which took nearly 1,200 people down with it, including 123 Americans. It had long been speculated that a second explosion that quickly sunk the boat was evidence of arms smuggling. The Lusitania was carrying millions of rounds and small arms weapons, which was not a secret, but it is now believed that the main explosion came from a boiler, not from explosive weaponry. Wilhelm later claimed he was appalled at the deaths and would not have approved an order firing on the ship if he had known that innocent passengers were aboard. On June 1, 1915, Wilhelm, fearing the entry of the U.S. into the war, issued an order that neutral ships be spared.

In the west, which was long considered the main theater of war for Wilhelm, the two sides were locked in a stalemate. Despite years of military planning that sought a quick victory in the west followed by a longer war in the east, forces in the west were bogged down in trenches that stretched for miles through France and Belgium. Meanwhile, the British remained in control of the English Channel and thus could resupply and reinforce the trench soldiers almost indefinitely.

As the highest adjudicator in the land, Kaiser Wilhelm was called upon to choose between contradictory war strategies put forward by rival factions within the army. The western front was commanded by Erich von Falkenhayn and his civilian counterpart Bethmann. Meanwhile, as Field Marshal Hindenburg and his quartermaster Ludendorff fought back the Tsar's forces on the eastern front in late 1914, they were also fighting political squabbles and trying to unseat Falkenhayn.

The effects of the squabbles between military leaders became apparent in the spring of 1915 while the Germans were driving back Russian troops. Hindenburg and Ludendorff both believed that victory was achievable if their forces were backed up with troops from the west; the two generals believed that they could force the Russians to sue for peace, leaving the entire army open to fight in the west. Falkenhayn, in contrast, felt that he should be given every available soldier to be prepared for the forthcoming crushing of the Allied line. In the end, in what Hindenburg later called the most difficult decision of the war, the Kaiser sided with Falkenhayn. It was believed the Tsar could be forced to negotiate only if the Russians were not only driven from Poland but if the Romanov dynasty capitulated. Even still, the Kaiser, while essentially supporting Falkenhayn's, strategy urged him to release some troops for a successful advance on the eastern front in the summer of 1915. Waged together with Austria, it reduced Russia's southern frontier to ruins, but despite the advances into Poland and the occupation of most of Belgium and a small part of France, the Germans were far from victory. In the beginning of 1915, the German use of chlorine gas on the western front was a great price to pay for so few gains, and the Germans were only able to maintain control of what they previously had without any offensive gains.

By the middle of the war, the Kaiser began a policy of watching and waiting. His navy moored at port because of British naval superiority, and the trench warfare was not producing movement. The Kaiser thought that Germany had to wait for the opportune moment to attack Britain, but other advisors, such as Admiral Tirpitz, believed a waiting period was bad for morale. He sought in vain to convince the Kaiser to continue unrestrained submarine warfare, and as 1916 was rung in, thoughtful observers were convinced the war could not be won. Among the public, patience was being lost; after a few quick victories in 1914, the public had become weary. With the daily sacrifices on the home front increasing rapidly, the public began to demand some sort of victory or a cessation of hostilities altogether.

As usual, the Kaiser tried to distill any question or problem into human terms, believing that his relationships with other individuals were all that was needed to secure a positive outcome. Long before the war, the history of Imperial Germany under the Kaiser had been shaped by the attempts made by courtiers to capture the Kaiser's ear or coax the Kaiser with sycophantic words into supporting the courtiers' plans, which could later be supported by presenting only good news on the topic. The Kaiser could be convinced that only he governed Germany, while in fact he was a mere figurehead. This was how the Kaiser operated before the war, and the war seems not to have changed that dynamic. During the war, the Kaiser continued to promote and listen to the people he liked regardless of outcome, and the worsening situation that Germany found itself in did not lead him to critique himself or his role in it.

One such change of circumstances that conspired to pit courtier against courtier occurred when Rumania entered the war on the side of the Allies. Convinced that this meant the end of the war because German troops would be needed to come to the aid of the Austrians, the Kaiser turned toward Hindenburg and Ludendorff, thinking that they were the only two people capable of waging the war on both fronts. Their popularity among the public was also no small measure in case Germany would have to sue for peace. With the resignation of Falkenhayne, any illusion that the Emperor was the chief warlord of the country was deflated; from this point forward, it was clear that Hindenburg and Ludendorff were the supreme war leaders. Ludendorff ended Falkenhayne's habit of hiding bad news from Wilhelm, and Ludendorff had little patience with the aristocratic courtiers that surrounded Wilhelm and sought to filter out bad news.

Taking over strategy against Rumania, two large German forces commanded by Falkenhayne overran Bucharest and occupied most of the kingdom. Brimming with optimism, the Kaiser awarded Hindenburg a special order of the Iron Cross, which had not been granted since the Napoleonic wars. Still, by 1916, the Kaiser had no choice but to reconsider the diplomatic preparations for the reintroduction of unrestricted submarine warfare. Wilhelm believed it was the only possible way to win the war, and alternatively the Kaiser considered the idea of suing for peace since the German army had possession of large areas of enemy land. In late 1916, he directed his new state secretary of the interior, Karl Halfferich, to contact President Woodrow Wilson. If the offer was made and Germany's enemies declined, it would give renewed energy to the claim that the only way to peace was through unrestricted submarine warfare.

In January 1917, Wilson urged Germany to enunciate peace conditions. Germany sought a return to the status quo, an increase in German colonial territory, and indemnities for the losses of the war. When the Allied powers rejected those terms, Wilhelm was free to wage war by any means necessary, and he signed an order that unrestricted submarine warfare was to commence on February 1.

Despite campaigning on his commitment to neutrality, President Wilson had been left with a tough decision by 1917. That year, the world learned that Germany was trying to coax Mexico into war against the United States. The Zimmerman Telegram, when Germany requested an alliance with Mexico against the United States, convinced Americans that Germany was indeed a threat to national security, and such a war would directly affect the U.S. homeland, which had not seen war since 1812. On top of that, with increasing hostilities between the two nations, the Germans vowed to return to a policy of unrestricted submarine warfare in the Atlantic. With that, Wilson requested a declaration of war from Congress, and received it on April 4, 1917. In his message to Congress, Wilson framed the war as a quest to make the world safe for democracy. The United States' mission, Wilson reassured Americans, was not to ally with Britain and France; instead, it would be an "associated" power, fighting its own, more idealistic, mission: the security of all people living in democratic countries. The federal government hired as many as 1,000,000 additional employees just to coordinate the production of food, materials, and soldiers to fight the war. Elsewhere, the Navy, which before the war had sufficient men to man only about 10% of its fleet, endured significant recruiting. The draft kicked in, and the U.S. ultimately mobilized over 4 million military personnel in the short period of less than one full year. The Selective Service Act, which instituted the draft, recruited about 2.5 million men alone.

Germany had calculated that the U.S. would be unable to mobilize and send men to Europe in less than 2 years, and they hoped to win the war before America could make a difference. Unrestricted submarine warfare was by any measure a success greater than predicted. Britain was beginning to feel the effects in foodstuffs just a month later, which forced the British to buy food from France, which was also running in short supply. Wilhelm was equally pleased with news of the downfall of the Russian Tsar, who abdicated power in March 1917. His successor announced that he would continue the war against the Central Powers, but Wilhelm believed the Russian Republic would not last long and seems not to have feared that the same chain of events were capable of happening in Germany. It was Bethmann who was much more concerned that events in Russia might prove a model to disaffected factions of Germans.

During the winter of 1916 and 1917, Wilhelm's authority within the executive was weakened by two developments. First, there was a drastic increase in power of the military leadership over the civilian government. The clash between Hindenburg and Ludendorff on the one side and chancellor Bethmann on the other increased until it was clear that Bethmann had to go. Also, throughout the war, after an initial "truce" known as the *Burgfrieden*, domestic developments unfolded that placed pressure of Wilhelm from both ends of the spectrum. On the left, a faction of the Social Democratic Party broke ranks and denounced the war. After 1916, there were increasing calls for rewards for the working class that was fighting in the trenches. On the right, an ultranationalist network with roots in the military called for annexations of neighboring territory and the rejection of any reforms called for by the Social Democratic Party. As the war dragged on without victory, Wilhelm's subjects began to acutely feel their sacrifices. Prices soared and food rationing was instituted. Starting in the spring of 1917, increasing shortages of food and the influence of the Russian revolution had created a very hostile situation.

French and British allies welcomed American forces with enthusiasm. After years of war, the Allied powers were tired and looked to their American counterparts for relief, and some movement in the quagmire. But for much of 1917, things went the Central Powers' way. The Bolshevik Revolution had led to Russia quitting the war, allowing the Germans to transfer soldiers to the Western front, and the Allied Powers had suffered a decisive defeat in the Nivelle Offensive of May 1917, as well as another defeat in November at the Battle of Caporetto in Slovenia. Incredibly, despite three years of being on the same side of the war, the French and British had not bothered to coordinate their commands until after those defeats; they finally formed a Supreme Council to coordinate their armies' movements and strategies.

To everyone's surprise the United States was sending an astounding 10,000 men a day over the Atlantic Ocean to Western Europe by the early spring of 1918, within less than a full year of mobilization. The nation had cut everyone's expectation in half, leading the sides to push for a more decisive ending immediately. The Germans began an offensive in March, a strategy crafted in part on the belief that American forces would be unprepared to arrive in Europe for another year. Germany hoped, therefore, to push Britain and France far enough back to eliminate them from the war, leading to a one-on-one with a subpar American military that Germany bet it could win.

Initially, the offensive broke through the Allied lines and pushed them to within less than 100 miles of Paris. However, at the Second Battle of the Marne, Germany only passed the Marne River for a brief time before being pushed back and defeated decisively by French forces. The results of the Spring Offensive were mixed for Germany: while it made modest territorial gains, its troops were severely depleted in the process. Before the Offensive, Germany had a strategic advantage over the Allies in terms of total soldier enlistments. That advantage was reduced to parity as a result of the failed Offensive.

The Germans found themselves right back where they started in July, but now facing the prospect of having to deal with hundreds of thousands of additional American troops. Thus began the final period of the war, the Hundred Days Offensive. After battles at Somme and Amiens, the Allied Powers were able to break the Hindenburg Line, moving rapidly towards Germany territory. The momentum was now clearly with the United States, with little Germany could do to turn the tide.

On November 11, 1918, the Germany army signed an armistice before the Allies entered German territory, and with that, the Great War was over. Much has been debated about Wilhelm's involvement in the decisions of war. Although the Kaiser appeared sidelined at times, research has shown that he was central in most issues of policy. The Kaiser did not play a creative role in the decisions of policy, and he was influenced by those around him, yet he was successful in making decisions when options were placed before him. He was also influential in his defense of ministers that fell out of favor with powerful forces. For example, it is unlikely that Falkenhayne could have remained in power as long as he did without the Kaiser's support.

After the war, Wilhelm spent 23 years in Dutch exile, an important period of time for historians because of two issues: his relationship with Jews and his attitude towards the National Socialists. Once settled in the Netherlands, Wilhelm spent his time reading and chopping wood and collaborating with publishers willing to promote a positive image of the former Kaiser. One of the central activities that emerged in his correspondence with publishers was the shifting of the blame for Germany's defeat onto particular people and groups. For example, Wilhelm claimed throughout the 1920s that the Weimar Republic had been created by Jews and paid for by Jewish money. Other statements share ideas of radical racial ideas later espoused by the National Socialists.

That said, it is overly simplistic to see Wilhelm as a precursor to Hitler, because the Kaiser's relationship toward the National Socialists was one of hostility and suspicion. In fact, after the persecution of Jews during Kristallnacht, the Kaiser claimed that he was "ashamed to be German" for the first time in his life. Furthermore, despite his anti-Semitism, he had long employed Jews, including shipbuilder Albert Ballin, banker Max Warburg, and coal magnate Eduard Arnhold. As Christopher Clark notes, Wilhelm's anti-Semitism was reactive – it peaked when the Wilhelm was under assault in the press or in public opinion. As Willibald Gutsche has detected, Wilhelm's increasing interest in the Jewish question was not an isolated event.

Bibliography

Balfour, Michael,,. The Kaiser and His Times,. Boston: Houghton Mifflin, 1964.

Cecil, Lamar,. Wilhelm II. Chapel Hill: University of North Carolina Press, 1989.

Goetz, Walter,. Kaiser Wilhelm II. Und Die Deutsche Geschichtsschreibung. München: Oldenbourg, 1955.

Tyler-Whittle,Michael Sidney,,. The Last Kaiser : A Biography of Wilhelm II, German Emperor and King of Prussia. New York: Times Books, 1977.

Van der Kiste, John,. Kaiser Wilhelm II : Germany's Last Emperor. Stroud: Sutton, 1999.

Made in the USA
Monee, IL
31 July 2021